your time-starved marriage

WORKBOOK FOR MEN

Resources by Les & Leslie Parrott
Books
 51 Creative Ideas for Marriage Mentors
 Becoming Soul Mates
 The Complete Guide to Marriage Mentoring
 Getting Ready for the Wedding
 I Love You More (and workbooks)
 Just the Two of Us
 Love Is . . .
 The Love List
 Love Talk (and workbooks)
 The Marriage Mentor Training Manual (for Husbands/Wives)
 Meditations on Proverbs for Couples
 Pillow Talk
 Questions Couples Ask
 Relationships (and workbook)
 Saving Your Marriage Before It Starts (and workbooks)
 Saving Your Second Marriage Before It Starts (and workbooks)

Video Curriculum — Zondervan*Groupware*®
 I Love You More
 Love Talk
 The Complete Resource Kit for Marriage Mentoring
 Relationships
 Saving Your Marriage Before It Starts

Audio Pages®
 Love Talk
 Relationships
 Saving Your Marriage Before It Starts
 Saving Your Second Marriage Before It Starts

Books by Les Parrott
 The Control Freak
 Helping Your Struggling Teenager
 High Maintenance Relationships
 The Life You Want Your Kids to Live
 Seven Secrets of a Healthy Dating Relationship
 Shoulda, Coulda, Woulda
 Once Upon a Family
 25 Ways to Win with People (coauthored with John Maxwell)
 Love the Life You Live (coauthored with Neil Clark Warren)

Books by Leslie Parrott
 If You Ever Needed Friends, It's Now
 You Matter More Than You Think
 God Loves You Nose to Toes (children's book)
 Marshmallow Clouds (children's book)

your
time-starved
marriage

WORKBOOK FOR MEN

how to stay connected at the speed of life

Drs. Les & Leslie Parrott

Authors of *Saving Your Marriage Before It Starts*

ZONDERVAN®

GRAND RAPIDS, MICHIGAN 49530 USA

ZONDERVAN.COM/
AUTHORTRACKER

ZONDERVAN®

Your Time-Starved Marriage Workbook for Men
Copyright © 2006 by Les and Leslie Parrott

Requests for information should be addressed to:

Zondervan, *Grand Rapids, Michigan 49530*

ISBN-10: 0-310-27155-X
ISBN-13: 978-0-310-27155-0

Published in association with Yates & Yates, LLP, Attorneys and Counselors, Suite 1000, Literary Agent, Orange, CA.

Interior design by Michelle Espinoza

Printed in the United States of America

09 10 11 12 • 18 17 16 15 14 13 12 11 10 9 8 7 6

contents

a letter from les

Popular columnist Hal Boyle once defined an "optimist" as a man who goes through life believing that somehow, somewhere, he will eventually arrive someplace on time — with his wife. He then added, "It never happens."

It doesn't take a psychologist to see that Hal probably had a few "time issues" with his wife. And to be honest, on occasion, I think I know how he felt. I suppose every husband does at some point. That's not to say that all wives run late. Not at all. It can be the husband who plays that role. But it is to say that more often than not, any particular husband and wife are going to differ in their perspectives on time. And once they understand these differences, they can use them to their advantage.

That's why I'm so glad you have chosen to use this workbook — whether it's to augment your reading of *Your Time-Starved Marriage* or to facilitate a small group experience you are doing with other couples. It says a lot about you, as a husband, that you are investing in your marriage in this way. Let's face it, we men sometimes get a bad rap for not wanting to "work on our marriage." But you obviously do want your marriage to be the best it can be. Through this workbook, I intend to help you do just that.

Why a Workbook?

Comedian Woody Allen said, "I took a speed-reading course and read *War and Peace* in twenty minutes. It involves Russia."

Ever felt like that after reading a book? Sometimes it becomes so easy to focus on finishing a book that we miss its main message. What you hold in your hand is an insurance policy against that happening while you are reading *Your Time-Starved Marriage*. But it's also more than that.

Books let us shake hands with new ideas, but these ideas remain as flat as the printed page if we do not apply them to our lives. For this reason, we have designed workbooks — one for you as a husband, and one for your wife — that will help you incorporate into your relationship the new lessons you learn while reading. And we've designed the workbook to be used either on your own or in a small group setting.

For Individual and Couple Study

As you read through the main book, you will discover a place at the end of each chapter where it points you to an exercise in this workbook. Most of the exercises are designed to take about five or ten minutes. You and your wife will usually work on them separately, then compare your results — that's why it's important to each have your own workbook. Or, you may sometimes work on an exercise together so you can put a new principle into practice. This is where real learning occurs and where new ideas become more than acquaintances; they begin to make a positive difference in your marriage.

We have used these exercises with countless couples, both in our counseling practice as well as in our seminar settings. They are proven and they work. And that's why we are passionate about your doing them as you read through our book. You just may find that the time you invest in doing these exercises with your wife pays some of the greatest dividends you could hope for.

While there is no one right way to use these workbooks, we suggest that you complete the exercises as you encounter them in the book, or soon after you have finished reading the chapter that covers the exercise. The point is to integrate the exercises into the process of reading the book.

For Small Group or Couple Study

In the latter section of this workbook you'll find a six-session small group study guide designed specifically for you and your wife to use with other couples.

I know, I know. You are probably cringing at the thought of talking about your marriage in front of other couples. Don't worry. This six-session study doesn't put anyone on the spot. You won't be forced to share something you don't want to. I've worked with countless men who are hesitant to participate in such a group, but once they try it, they soon see just how painless — and positive — it can be.

Speaking to you, man to man, I highly recommend that you give a small group study of this topic some consideration. Participating in a small group with a few other couples is far easier than you might guess. And you will be giving your wife one of the best gifts she'll receive all year.

Not only that, but research shows that one of the most effective ways of internalizing new content and gaining new insight is by discussing the material with others. And when it comes to learning more about time management in marriage, this is especially true. That's why we've designed a DVD kit for just such a purpose. It includes six video sessions with conversational jump starters and lots of practical application to help your group get the most from *Your Time-Starved Marriage*. To find out more about the kit, visit your local bookstore or check our website at *www.RealRelationships. com.*

Whether you are using these workbooks individually as a couple or in a small group setting, we hope you'll make the material your own as you proceed through these pages. Don't get too hung up on following the rules. If a particular exercise leads you down a more intriguing path, take it. Some of these exercises may simply serve as springboards to discussions that better fit your style. However, if an exercise seems challenging, don't give up on it. As the saying goes, anything worth having is worth working for—especially when it comes to your marriage.

So, whether you are a speed-reader or not, we hope you don't approach *Your Time-Starved Marriage Workbook* as just another item to check off your "to-do" list. We hope and pray that you will instead use these exercises, self-tests, and discussion questions to internalize the book's message and fortify your relationship by reclaiming the moments you've been missing together.

Les Parrott
Seattle, Washington

part one

exercises

maximizing
your time quotient

Use the circle on the following page (or draw it on scratch paper) to design a personal pie chart of how you and your wife use your time together. List the activities you are likely to do in a typical week. For example, your list might include household chores, but write down only those you do together. Other items may include grocery shopping, taking walks, exercising, watching television or DVDs, eating out, dining in, playing with your children, talking on the phone, having sex, talking face-to-face, gardening, and attending church. Consider every possible activity you share in your waking hours in an average week and then designate the amount of the pie to that activity as it fits. Don't worry about making it perfect. And don't hesitate to have some tiny slivers of activities you share that are a part of your "time pie." This is just a quick way to help you see how you spend your time together.

By the way, don't try to guess what you think your wife wants you to include. Be honest. Think of every activity you can that you share with your wife.

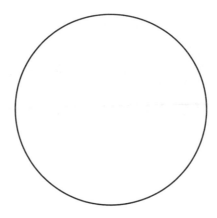

How Do Your Hours Stack Up?

- Estimate the number of hours this pie chart represents in your typical week. In other words, how many hours per week do the two of you spend together? _____

- Are you satisfied with the amount of quality time you spend together, or would you like more? In other words, identify the best times you share together.

_____

_____

_____

What Matters Most to You?

- Okay, here's the tough part. As you look at the activities represented by the slices of your pie chart, what are the top half dozen or so activities that you prize the most?

_____

_____

_____

_____

_____

_____

Putting Yourself in Your Wife's Shoes

- Before you share your answers to these questions with your wife, take a moment to consider how she may have answered these items. In general, men typically report being less troubled about "sharing time together" than their wives. Do you think this is true of you? Why or why not? And if there was one positive message you would like to express to your wife as you begin this study on "your time-starved marriage," what would it be? Take a moment to jot it down here. And focus on what you can say that would lift her spirits.

    As we begin this study together, I want you to know . . .

  _____

  _____

  _____

Make Time to Talk about This Together

- Now, compare your responses to those of your wife. Talk about what you can do to maximize these activities. What can you do, in other words, to increase the amount of time you have to enjoy these things that are most important to you as a couple? Hint: Part of the answer may be found in identifying activities in your life that can be reduced—even those activities you may do together that neither of you really enjoys. We'll revisit this idea of making more quality time and give you practical ways to do so. For now, what comes to your mind for maximizing these activities?

_____

_____

_____

exercise two

is your marriage
slipping into the future?

Tim Allen, star of the television sitcom *Home Improvement*, said, "How much of the day are you awake? You think, 'I've gotta get that dry cleaning, I gotta get this going, and this, and this.' All of a sudden it's dinnertime. And then there's a moment of connection with your spouse ... Then you read and go to bed. Wake up and then it's the same all over. You're not awake, you're not living, you're not experiencing."[1]

Have you fallen asleep in your marriage? Are you stuck in a rut of doing errands and other mundane tasks, all to wake up the next morning and go through the same motions again? The following self-test will help you assess your marriage.

Do you ...

1. Sometimes finish your wife's sentences?	Y	N
2. Find yourself rushing when there's no reason to?	Y	N
3. Spend less than thirty minutes in meaningful conversation with your wife each day?	Y	N
4. Realize you haven't expressed gratitude to your wife in days?	Y	N

1. "Self-Improvement," *Reader's Digest*, October 2001, 86.

5. Feel like you're waiting to live until you reach a certain milestone?   Y   N

6. Have a tough time separating work life from home life?   Y   N

7. Feel like you and your wife are the two proverbial ships passing in the night?   Y   N

8. Feel your "together time" has been on hold even though it is "just around the corner"?   Y   N

9. Find that too many of your conversations with your wife center on schedules and tasks?   Y   N

10. Sometimes view work as an escape from your hectic home life?   Y   N

How'd You Answer?

If you answered yes to more than a couple of these items, you're probably living in a time-starved marriage. But don't fret. You're not alone. Not by a long shot. Even if you answered yes to a majority of these items, you're not alone. We can all use a little home improvement when it comes to managing our time together.

Make Time to Talk about This

After each of you has truthfully answered these ten questions, compare notes. Which items do you agree or disagree on and why? Don't use this conversation to prove a point. Use it to more accurately understand your wife. In other words, don't pick apart her answer; instead, genuinely try to understand what she is saying. The more you see life from her perspective, the easier your life — and your marriage — become.

eliminating hurry from your marriage

What would you do if your marriage literally depended upon eliminating hurry from your home? If you knew your marriage wouldn't make it another year unless you seriously curbed busyness from your life, what would you do?

We know it's a dramatic question. But sometimes a question like this can get us to think more intensely and drill down more deeply on an issue. So, how would you go about the task of eliminating busyness from your marriage? List everything you can think of in the space below or on a piece of scratch paper. Don't worry about how rational or irrational one of your ideas is—just jot it down.

_____

_____

_____

_____

_____

Now, compare your answers to those of your wife and talk about how realistic or unrealistic each idea is. Give yourselves a few minutes to discuss them. Then on your own, select the top three ideas from your joint list that you each think could be done and could make a positive difference. Again, compare your answers. You may find that you simply don't agree on some of them, but chances are you will agree on at least one of them. And that's a place to start. Write it down here.

One thing we both agree we can do to eliminate hurry from our home is to ...

_____

_____

_____

Congratulations. You now have something you will actually put into practice to slow down your pace together. Make a pact to come back to this agreement a week from now and assess how well you are doing to carry it out and what difference it has made. Once it becomes a habit, you may want to revisit your brainstorm of other ideas and add a second solution to eliminate hurry.

are you fast or slow?

This simple exercise is a quick and easy way to consider where the two of you are on the most fundamental of time continuums: fast versus slow. We'll follow it up with a few application questions related more directly to the chapter's content.

Take a moment to simply circle the descriptor in each of these eight pairings that best describes you on most days.

1. Busy   Calm
2. Controlling   Careful
3. Aggressive   Receptive
4. Hurried   Unhurried
5. Stressed   Still
6. Impatient   Patient
7. Active   Reflective
8. Quantity-over-quality   Quality-over-quantity

Add up the qualities you circled in each column. Which column outweighs the other and by how much? The qualities on the left side are obviously associated with being "fast-paced," while those on the right are "slow-paced."

• • •

Discuss your answers together:

- Are you satisfied with your self-assessment? Why or why not?

  _____

  _____

  _____

- Which of these descriptors do you want to incorporate more into your life?

  _____

  _____

  _____

- What do your answers reveal about you in comparison to your wife? As a man, do you think there is a fundamental gender difference at play here, or does it have more to do with your personalities?

  _____

  _____

  _____

Also:

- Once you have both taken the online Time-Style Marriage Assessment (TSMA), discuss your results together. And remember, this little assessment is painless. There are no "right" or "wrong" answers, and it only takes about five minutes. And it's free! You won't want to miss out on this helpful resource.

exercise five

how to make
more quality time

Consider a scenario. You have twenty-four one-dollar bills in your pocket. Each of them represents an hour in your day. As each hour elapses, you turn in one of your bills. Which hour is the best deal? In other words, which hour was best spent? Which hour was well worth it? Did it involve your wife? Your kids? If not, that's fine. Maybe it was something exciting at work. Or maybe it was a precious hour of sleep you especially needed. If you use this scenario to reflect on how you spent your time yesterday, which hour would you say was best spent?

_____

_____

Now consider some time that you didn't experience in the past day — time you would have liked to have spent with your wife. Is there something you would have enjoyed doing with her? Something you didn't get to do because there wasn't enough time? What would that be? It may be as simple as a few minutes to check in with each other on how the day went. Or it may be lingering leisurely over coffee. Or working in the garden together. Or taking a long walk. Note it in the space provided on the following page.

_____

_____

_____

Next, consider how many of your twenty-four dollars you'd be willing to sacrifice tomorrow for that time you missed out on with your wife today. In other words, how much time are you willing to sacrifice from other activities in order to have more of that kind of time you just noted above? Would it take making another ten minutes in your day? Twenty minutes? Another hour or two? Determine the amount of time you need to make for that activity, and write it here: _____

Okay. Now you've determined the amount of quality time you'd like to make. The only thing left is deciding where in your day you are going to take that time from. What are your options? Is it the time it takes to prepare dinner? The time you spend on errands? The time you spend watching TV or reading the paper? Housekeeping? Volunteering? Lying on the couch? Or is it some of your sleep time? Review the first exercise you did in this workbook (your "time pie") to help you here. Identify the time you'd be willing to sacrifice tomorrow in order to have the quality time you crave with your wife, and write it here:

_____

_____

_____

Now, to help you better empathize with your wife on this exercise, consider what you think might be the most difficult sacrifice she might have to make (from her perspective) to have more quality time with you, and write it here:

_____

_____

_____

Now, check in with her to see how accurate you are. If you're way off, that's okay. The point is to empathize by seeing this from her perspective.

There you have it. To make more quality time, you've got to give up time you are now giving to secondary causes. It's that simple. And that difficult. It's a sacrifice. But that's what priorities are all about, sacrificing something else you might enjoy for the greater good. We remind you of what Robert McKain said: "The reason most goals are not achieved is that we spend our time doing second things first." Put first things first tomorrow — and every day — in your marriage.

making your mundane moments count

What can you do to prepare your mind for the little but important moments you've been missing together? Below is a list of common moments, times when we are likely to connect with each other. They are also times that too often slip right by us without much thought or intention. Consider each item and rate how well you do it.

Saying hello ...

Not Very Well   Extremely Well

1   2   3   4   5   6   7   8   9   10

Saying good-bye ...

Not Very Well   Extremely Well

1   2   3   4   5   6   7   8   9   10

Saying good-night ...

Not Very Well   Extremely Well

1   2   3   4   5   6   7   8   9   10

Saying good morning ...

Not Very Well   Extremely Well

1   2   3   4   5   6   7   8   9   10

Saying thanks ...

Not Very Well   Extremely Well

1   2   3   4   5   6   7   8   9   10

Saying I'm sorry ...

Not Very Well   Extremely Well

1   2   3   4   5   6   7   8   9   10

Saying I care about you ...

Not Very Well   Extremely Well

1   2   3   4   5   6   7   8   9   10

Saying I understand ...

Not Very Well   Extremely Well

1   2   3   4   5   6   7   8   9   10

Saying I love you ...

Not Very Well   Extremely Well

1   2   3   4   5   6   7   8   9   10

Now review those items you ranked at a four or less. Talk to each other about why you ranked them the way you did. What can you do to be more mindful of these common moments? In other words, as a husband, how can you become more invested and present in each of them? By doing so, by giving them some forethought, you're much more likely to make them meaningful when they happen. So choose two of the items and focus on them in the week ahead.

beating back your time bandits

As you just learned, stealing back your time comes down to choices. So in this simple exercise we want to help you consider a few choices that may change the course of your marriage. Or at the very least, they might change how much time you reclaim for your marriage.

We want you to begin by taking inventory of what robs you of your time. Your time stealers may be the ones we talked about in this chapter, or they may be something specific to your situation. And they are likely to be different from your wife's. Whatever they are, note what has swiped too much of your time together in the past week:

Husband	Wife

Now take a moment to discuss your separate answers. Why did you choose the time bandits you did? What are some recent examples of how they robbed your marriage? Are your answers in agreement with your wife's? Why or why not?

With these time bandits identified, consider what choices you could make to take back this stolen time. How could you get this culprit to surrender what it's taking from you?

We can't give you the answer because this is a personal choice, but to help you get started, consider this example.

Say technology is your time tyrant. You could choose to have a weekly media fast. On an agreed-upon day each week, you could choose to have an evening at home where you turn off the television, shut down your computers, and unplug the phones (including cells and beepers). If technology is your primary time bandit, this single choice would dramatically put more time back into your marriage. You'd probably even breathe deeper on this evening — as long as you don't allow the time you create to be swallowed by some other lurking bandit that keeps you apart.

Of course, a "media fast" may be much tougher for you than it would be for your wife (I know that this is the case in my home), so consider what choices could be made that would be equally challenging for both of you.

You get the idea. So talk to each other — in very specific terms — about making one practical choice right now that would put more time back into your marriage because it would be a blow to one of the time bandits you identified above.

- What's the choice?

_____

_____

_____

_____

- How realistic is it?

_____

_____

_____

_____

- When can you put it into practice?

_____

_____

_____

_____

enjoying the rare delicacy of slow food

Some couples find it enjoyable to cook together. We're not one of them, but we do enjoy a slow-paced meal. So for us, we're most likely to have our unhurried meal at a nice, quiet restaurant. Every couple finds their own way to share a slow meal. This exercise is designed to get you talking about it. There are no right or wrong answers, just questions to discuss.

- When would you say was the last time the two of you had a slow-paced meal with no television or other distractions?
  - ❏ This week
  - ❏ This month
  - ❏ This year
  - ❏ Can't remember

- How prone are you to sabotage a potential slow-paced meal by replacing it with fast food?
  - ❏ Most days
  - ❏ Once a week
  - ❏ Less than once a month
  - ❏ Almost never

- If you are prone to fast food, why would you say you are most likely to indulge?
  - ❑ It's cheap.
  - ❑ It's fast.
  - ❑ It's easy.
  - ❑ It's fun (for the kids).

- How might your idea of a slow-paced meal differ from your wife's?

  _____

  _____

- Would you like to have more slow-paced meals together, or are you doing well in this area already? Why or why not?

  _____

  _____

- When would the two of you be most likely to enjoy a slow-paced meal together? Is there a certain day of the week that works best?

  _____

  _____

- What's your favorite part of having an unhurried mealtime together?

  _____

  _____

money talks
and so can we

The time mine of money will only pay off when you begin to talk about your finances in relationship to your time. This exercise is designed to help you drill down on this topic and explore it together.

Since money is typically the most common source of conflict for most couples, we want to begin by pinpointing where this is especially true for the two of you. What's the primary source of your financial friction with each other? Rate yourselves on the following:

How we spend and save differently from one another ...

Not a problem   Definitely a problem

1 2 3 4 5 6 7 8 9 10

Our financial debt and/or lack of savings ...

Not a problem   Definitely a problem

1 2 3 4 5 6 7 8 9 10

Unclear roles (who is to pay the bills, etc.) ...

Not a problem   Definitely a problem

1 2 3 4 5 6 7 8 9 10

Of course, you may know that your financial friction stems from another source entirely. Whatever it is, what can the two of you do, right now, to improve your circumstances? Be specific. And if you were to remedy the situation right now, how much time do you believe you would salvage for your relationship?

_____

_____

_____

_____

Next, tell yourself the truth about your money and where it is going. This will take some time. For the next five days, keep a spending journal if you think it will be helpful. It's easy. Just go to *www.RealRelationships.com*, click on "Time-Starved Marriage Tools," and you'll have all you need to get started today.

At the end of each day, review the receipts you stuffed in your pocket and write down everything you bought and how much it cost—from newspapers and packs of gum, to bills and clothing. At the end of five days, add up your entries to see how much you spent. What could you have cut out? Were they all necessary, well-thought-out purchases, or are you a compulsive spender? More importantly, how can this information help you redeem time that is being wasted because of how you treat your finances?

Finally, talk about how you, as a man, feel about money. We know from research that many men unconsciously, if not consciously, believe they are what they make. How about you? Does money factor into your feelings of self-worth? How does this play a role in how you spend your time? Have you ever talked to your wife about this? If not, this is a great time to do so.

exercise ten

getting real about r & r

If we only stop to rest when we are finished with all our work, we will never stop. Work always abounds. It's never completely done. So in this final exercise, we want to help you take a deliberate rest from all your toil. We want you to consider the three Rs and how they relate to your relationship.

Rest: Taking Time for Sweet, Sweet Slumber

Some couples are often at odds about sleep. One of them thinks the other doesn't get enough sleep, for example. How about the two of you?

- Ideally, how many hours of sleep do you need each night?

- Realistically, how many hours of sleep do you get? _____

- Do you think your spouse gets enough sleep? Yes No

How would you rate the quality of your sleep?

Tossing and Turning   Sleep Like a Baby

1   2   3   4   5   6   7   8   9   10

How would you rate your spouse's quality of sleep?

Tossing and Turning   Sleep Like a Baby

1   2   3   4   5   6   7   8   9   10

Take a moment to discuss your answers to these questions. Explore what you can do to help each other sleep more soundly.

Next, explore what you might learn from your dreams tonight. Decide to remember what you dream. Sounds funny, but experiments have shown that simply being motivated to recall your dreams really does improve your powers of recall. It also helps to have a notepad and pen by your bed to write down what you dreamed. So, to maximize your slumber and to join your spirits, keep a brief dream journal. For the next few days note your dreams and talk about them together. What do you think they mean? What do they have to say about whatever's on your mind? Do they shed any light on your relationship?

Recreation: Getting Serious about Having Fun

Make a list of the things you do for recreation together as a couple. Understandably, what may be fun to you may not be as fun for your wife. For now, that's okay. Just list a half dozen of the things you especially enjoy:

_____

_____

_____

_____

_____

_____

Now, how many of those activities on your list have the two of you done in the last month? If you're not doing these activities as often as you'd like, all you have to do is pick one activity, do it, pick another, do it ... you get the idea. Sometimes it just takes an ounce of initiative to get you going.

Restoration: Making Your Sabbath a Retreat for Your Soul

Imagine taking a cost-free vacation once a week with no errands to run, no bills to pay, no nagging feeling that your to-do list is not being adequately diminished. Computer and TV screens remain dark, ringing phones are ignored, and all the whirs and hums of the 24/7 world come to a halt. A pipe dream? Maybe. But it's reality for millions of couples who take their Sabbath seriously.

Take inventory of your Sundays over the past four weeks. What's your routine? Do you feel more rested, more at peace, more attuned to God as a result of the way you spend your Sundays? Are your spirits joined closer together as husband and wife as a result of your Sabbath? Or is it just another day? In the space below note a couple of specific and realistic steps the two of you can take to make next Sunday more meaningful and truly restful.

_____

_____

_____

_____

part two

for group or couple discussion with the dvd curriculum

introduction

Studying this material in a small group with other couples is one of the best ways to make it stick — and have a lot of fun in the process. To that end, we've created this six-session small group discussion guide. Why six sessions? Because most groups feel that six sessions is just about the right length for a small group series. Though we've created this discussion guide for group use, it is also adaptable for individual couple's study.

Before your group meetings, it would be helpful for you to read the chapters associated with the session, but this is not required. After all, this is a group for "time-starved" couples! So if you can make time to read the chapters, great! If not, don't worry. We understand if you've been short on time! You can still join in on the discussion (it doesn't rely on having read the chapters), and you don't need to feel an ounce of guilt. The purpose is to enjoy the interaction and to learn from it. You can always read the chapters later, if you wish.

Here's a quick glimpse at what you'll be doing in each small group session. We've designed each session to last about an hour, but you can take more or less time as your schedule dictates.

Just for Fun (5 minutes)

Each session begins with a question that is "just for fun" — a kind of icebreaker. We've selected the questions from our book *Love Talk Starters*, which contains about three hundred questions. They are just to get the wheels turning and to help you connect as you come together as a group. You can order this little book of questions at *www.RealRelationships.com.*

Video Notes (10 – 15 minutes)

In addition to hearing from Les and Leslie Parrott, each session will include a brief video featuring several real-life couples who are exploring these issues just as you are. As you watch the DVD, feel free to jot down your notes, questions, and reactions in the space provided.

Talking about Time (30 minutes)

The list of questions you'll find in this section is designed to spark ideas, reactions, and real-life examples. You'll notice that some are the same as the "For Reflection" questions at the end of each chapter, so you will have a chance to think about the questions before you engage in them as a group.

As you interact, remember that a key ingredient to successful small group discussion is vulnerability. This doesn't mean you have to say anything you don't want to. It's just that, typically, the more transparent you are, the more meaningful the experience will be, and the more open others will be as well. Vulnerability begets vulnerability. However, we caution you not to use this time to gripe about your wife in some way. Don't embarrass each other by dragging out dirty laundry you know would upset your wife. You want to be genuine and vulnerable, but not at the expense of your wife's feelings.

Another key ingredient in these discussions is specificity. You'll gain much more out of this time when you use specific examples with each other. So with this in mind, we will remind you to "be specific" every so often.

Finally, if you are a small group facilitator, don't feel that you need to follow the order given or even use every question. Let the dynamics of the discussion be your guide.

Talking Through Your Workbook Exercise (10 minutes)

Each of the sessions will rely on an exercise from this workbook. You will typically spend time within the group session doing the exercise, then discussing it. We've selected exercises that will not put anyone on the spot or force anyone to share information they don't want to. Of course, your group may elect to use other exercises from this workbook to discuss if you wish. That's up to you and your group.

Making Time Together as a Couple

Finally, we've included suggestions for ways you can take this small group experience into your week together as a couple. We encourage you to further discuss and apply the material as a way to connect and grow together. And of course, you can also read the book together or individually if you can make the time. Again, no pressure or guilt.

One more thing. Relax. Have fun. And learn all you can to reclaim the moments you've been missing together.

right here, right now — is your marriage slipping into the future?

This session is based on chapters 1 and 2 in *Your Time-Starved Marriage*. However, reading these chapters before or after you participate in this session is optional.

Just for Fun (5 minutes)

Tell the group about one timepiece (a watch or a clock) you own or have owned in the past that has particular meaning to you and why. Or show the group the watch you are currently wearing and comment on how it reflects your personality.

Video Notes (10–15 minutes)

_____

_____

_____

_____

_____

_____

Talking about Time (30 minutes)

1. Do you know the experience of rushing around to get more done more quickly, only to find that you seem to have less time on your hands? If so, why do you think this happens?

_____

_____

_____

_____

2. Little has been written about how to manage time as a married couple. Do you have any hunches as to why? What's the best advice on time management as a couple that you've ever received?

_____

_____

_____

_____

3. How will you know when you are maximizing your moments together? Be specific and concrete.

_____

_____

_____

_____

4. In what ways have you spent your life "indefinitely preparing to live"? In other words, when have you more or less put your life on hold until a specific milestone was met? If you could do it over again, how might you do it differently?

_____

_____

_____

_____

5. As you review your past week, what choices have you made to maximize your time in ways that are meaningful (not necessarily productive) to you?

_____

_____

_____

_____

Talking Through Your Workbook Exercise (10 minutes)

Within your small group, take time to complete exercise 1 ("Maximizing Your Time Quotient") in your workbook. It helps you plot exactly how you spend your time together and how you might like to prioritize or maximize that time.

After you have completed the exercise, take a couple minutes to compare notes as a couple and then come back together as a group and share what you have learned in doing this exercise.

Making Time Together as a Couple

Spend some time in the days ahead, just the two of you, completing exercise 2 ("Is Your Marriage Slipping into the Future?"). It will help you "snap out of it" if you happen to be stuck in a time rut.

Also, spend some time this week, just the two of you, talking about your small group session. What did you learn from other couples in the discussion this week? As a husband, what did you learn from any of the other men in the group? After reviewing the content of chapters 1 and 2 in the book, identify the most important "takeaway" you gained from studying this topic this week.

_____

_____

_____

_____

busyness — the archenemy of every marriage

This session is based on chapter 3 in *Your Time-Starved Marriage*. Again, reading this chapter, while very helpful, is not required for participating in the group.

Just for Fun (5 minutes)

Poet E. E. Cummings once said, "The most wasted of all days is one without laughter." When was the last time the two of you enjoyed a good laugh together? What was so funny?

Video Notes (10–15 minutes)

_____

_____

_____

_____

_____

_____

Talking about Time (30 minutes)

1. What makes you feel most busy? In what areas of your life do you most often feel that you must pedal faster and faster to keep up? Why?

    _____

    _____

    _____

    _____

2. Busyness can negatively affect four areas: your conversations, your love life, your ability to have fun, and your spirituality. Which of these four areas is most negatively affected by your busyness? Why?

    _____

    _____

    _____

    _____

3. After reviewing the arsenal of ways to battle busyness in this chapter, what is the one you feel can be most useful to both of you? How and when you will put it into practice?

    _____

    _____

    _____

    _____

Talking Through Your Workbook Exercise (10 minutes)

Within your small group, take time to complete exercise 3 ("Eliminating Hurry from Your Marriage") in your workbook. The exercise will help you determine what you would do if your marriage literally depended upon eliminating hurry from your home.

After you have completed the exercise, take a couple minutes to compare notes as a couple and then come back together as a group and share what you have learned in doing this exercise.

Before you end your small group session this week, decide together whether you would each like to take the free online Time-Style Marriage Assessment (TSMA) at *www.RealRelationships.com*. It will take just five minutes, and you would bring your printed results from the online assessment to discuss the following week. By the way, the TSMA is not something you pass or fail — it simply describes your unique approach to time. We highly recommend that you use this free online resource that is designed specifically for this purpose.

Making Time Together as a Couple

Spend some time this week, just the two of you, talking about your small group session. What did you learn from other couples this week? Also, review the content of chapter 3 in the book, then identify the most important "takeaway" you gained from studying this topic.

_____

_____

_____

_____

time styles — uncovering your unique approach to time

This session is based on chapter 4 in *Your Time-Starved Marriage*.

Just for Fun (5 minutes)

Identify one quality (it doesn't need to be the most important), trait, or behavior you admire, respect, or appreciate in the couple seated on your right. Say what it is and why you admire it. Or, if you and your wife are discussing this on your own, name a quality you admire in another couple you both know.

Video Notes (10 – 15 minutes)

_____

_____

_____

_____

_____

_____

_____

Talking about Time (30 minutes)

1. Are you more subjective (unscheduled) or objective (scheduled) when it comes to experiencing time, and why?

_____

_____

_____

_____

2. Are you more present oriented or future oriented in where you focus your energy? What's your reasoning?

_____

_____

_____

_____

3. Of the four time styles—Accommodator, Dreamer, Planner, or Processor—which one do you most identify with? In which camp do you see your wife tending to land? How would you describe your combination of time styles (what are its strengths and challenges)?

_____

_____

_____

_____

Talking Through Your Workbook Exercise (10 minutes)

Within your last small group session, you may have chosen to take the free online Time-Style Marriage Assessment (TSMA) at *www.RealRelationships.com*. If you all agreed to do this, discuss your findings — both your individual styles and how your time styles mix as a couple. Share the diagram of your time style with the group.

If for some reason you were not all able to take the TSMA as a group or chose not to, take time to complete exercise 4 ("Are You Fast or Slow?") in your workbook. It provides another snapshot of how the two of you may differ in approaching time. After you have completed the exercise, take a couple minutes to compare notes as a couple and then come back together as a group and share what you have learned in doing this exercise.

Making Time Together as a Couple

Spend some time this week, just the two of you, talking about your small group session. What did you learn this week from other couples in your group? Also, review the content of chapter 4 in the book, then identify the most important "takeaway" you gained from studying this topic together. And if your group didn't take the online TSMA, be sure to do that on your own this week.

prioritizing prime time — maximizing your moments

This session is based on chapters 5 and 6 in *Your Time-Starved Marriage*.

Just for Fun (5 minutes)

As a couple, you are appointed by the president of the United States to be the first ever Secretary of Enjoyment. Your job is to bring more fun into the lives of everyday Americans. What's your first tactical priority?

Video Notes (10–15 minutes)

_____

_____

_____

_____

_____

_____

Talking about Time (30 Minutes)

1. A major step toward "making more time" is to put first things first and do what matters most. Why can it be so difficult to set your priorities and allow them to direct your decisions?

_____

_____

_____

_____

2. Identify a specific time when you felt like your priorities got out of whack — when you were distracted — and as a result you ended up wasting or misusing your time. Looking back, what caused the distraction and, more importantly, what can you do to safeguard yourself from having this happen again?

_____

_____

_____

_____

3. What's one thing that you could leave "undone" for a while? Something that would give you more time together if it was not accomplished, and it would be okay?

_____

_____

_____

_____

4. Recall an experience together from a year ago or so that you still hold as a meaningful moment. What made it so and why, specifically, is it still in your memory bank?

_____

_____

_____

_____

5. When you consider otherwise mundane moments in your marriage, which one of these times holds the most promise for you and your wife to connect: saying hello, saying good-bye, having pillow talk before you fall asleep, or when you're having a tough day?

_____

_____

_____

_____

6. What marital routine or ritual helps you to connect?

_____

_____

_____

_____

Talking Through Your Workbook Exercise (10 minutes)

Within your small group, take time to complete exercise 6 ("Making Your Mundane Moments Count") in your workbook. It will help you pinpoint what routines of life you might be able to make more meaningful.

After you have completed the exercise, take a couple minutes to compare notes as a couple and then come back together as a group and share what you have learned in doing this exercise.

Making Time Together as a Couple

Spend some time this week, just the two of you, completing exercise 5 ("How to Make More Quality Time"). It will augment the exercise you did in your small group. Also, discuss what you learned this week from other couples in your group. After reviewing the content of chapters 5 and 6 in the book, identify the most important "takeaway" you gained from studying this topic.

time bandits — catching your time stealers red-handed

This session is based on chapter 7 in *Your Time-Starved Marriage.*

Just for Fun (5 minutes)

If your small group were cast in a movie about an elaborate jewel heist, what roles would each of you play: the mastermind thief, the getaway driver, the safe cracker, the unsuspecting jeweler, the suspicious detective, the police chief, or the double-crossing thief who switches the jewels? Why?

Video Notes (10 – 15 minutes)

Talking about Time (30 minutes)

1. Do you agree that unfinished business from your past can steal time from your present? If you feel comfortable sharing with the group, discuss what you have done to bring closure to unfinished business in your own life.

    _____

    _____

    _____

    _____

2. In what specific ways has technology — those electronic gizmos designed to save us more time — ended up stealing your time? Does technology sometimes delude you into thinking you're saving time for your marriage when just the opposite is happening? If so, how?

    _____

    _____

    _____

    _____

3. When are you most likely to become impatient and why? When has your impatience actually ended up costing you more time than you thought it might save you?

    _____

    _____

_____

_____

Talking Through Your Workbook Exercise (10 minutes)

Within your small group, take time to complete exercise 7 ("Beating Back Your Time Bandits") in your workbook. It will help you identify your time bandits, then come up with strategies for protecting the time you treasure.

After you have completed the exercise, take a couple minutes to compare notes as a couple and then come back together as a group and share what you have learned in doing this exercise.

Making Time Together as a Couple

Spend some time this week, just the two of you, talking about your small group session. What did you learn from other couples this week? Also, review the content of chapter 7 in the book, then identify the most important "takeaway" you gained from studying this topic.

_____

_____

_____

time mines — where you're sure to strike gold

This session is based on chapters 8, 9, and 10 in *Your Time-Starved Marriage*.

Just for Fun (5 minutes)

If the two of you, as a couple, were gold miners and you struck it rich, what would you do with your million-dollar fortune if you had to spend it all on other people you've never met and never will? Why?

Video Notes (10–15 minutes)

_____

_____

_____

_____

_____

_____

_____

Talking about Time (30 minutes)

1. What were mealtimes like at your house as a kid and how do they differ from what you do today? How has that impacted your time together as a couple versus the kind of time your parents had together?

    _____

    _____

    _____

2. If you could press a magic button to make your mealtimes what you'd like them to be, what would happen? How much of your ideal could you make a reality by what you bring to the table—literally?

    _____

    _____

    _____

3. Would you rather have an extra hour at home each day or an extra ten thousand dollars? Why?

    _____

    _____

    _____

4. What's the most fun recreational activity you enjoy as a couple when you have the time for it? What other activities do you enjoy together and how can you, in specific terms, create more time to enjoy them?

your time-starved marriage

_____

_____

_____

Talking Through Your Workbook Exercise (10 minutes)

Within your small group, take time to complete exercise 8 ("Enjoying the Rare Delicacy of Slow Food") in your workbook. It focuses on helping you enjoy a slow-cooked conversation over a meal together—one of the often neglected "time mines" of marriage.

After you have completed the exercise, take a few minutes to compare notes as a couple and then come back together as a group and share what you have learned in doing this exercise.

Making Time Together as a Couple

Spend some time this week, just the two of you, completing exercise 9 ("Money Talks and So Can We"). Discussing your personal money matters in front of a group is enough to make most anyone nervous, but don't let that keep you from talking about it as a couple. You'll be amazed how much time you can save by getting your finances squared away. And exercise 10 ("Getting Real about R & R") will be a nice way to explore what the two of you can do at a practical level to bring more rest and relaxation into your relationship. Finally, take some time to talk about what the two of you gained from being involved in this small group study. What will be your most important takeaways?

_____

_____

_____

We hope you've enjoyed your small group experience.
We'd love to hear from you.
To provide feedback and to learn about
additional small group kits by Les and Leslie Parrott,
visit www.RealRelationships.com.

Your Time-Starved Marriage

How to Stay Connected at the Speed of Life

Drs. Les and Leslie Parrott

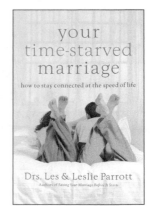

This is not a book about being more productive —it's a book about being more connected as a couple. In *Your Time-Starved Marriage*, Drs. Les and Leslie Parrott show how you can create a more fulfilling relationship with time—and with each other.

The moments you miss together are gone forever. Irreplaceable. And yet, until now, there has not been a single book for couples on how to better manage and reclaim this priceless resource. The Parrotts show you how to take back the time you've been missing together—and maximize the moments you already have. *Your Time-Starved Marriage* shows you how to

- relate to time in a new way as a couple
- understand the two lies every time-starved couple so easily believes
- slay the "busyness" giant that threatens your relationship
- integrate your time-style with a step-by-step approach that helps you make more time together
- stop the "time bandits" that steal your minutes
- maximize mealtime, money time, and leisure time
- reclaim all the free time you've been throwing away

Learn to manage your time together more than it manages you. Dramatically improve your ability to reclaim the moments you've been missing. *Your Time-Starved Marriage* gives you tools to feed your time-starved relationship, allowing you to maximize the moments you have together and enjoy them more.

Hardcover   0-310-24597-4

Also Available:

0-310-81053-1	*Time Together*	Hardcover
0-310-26885-0	*Your Time-Starved Marriage*	Audio CD, Unabridged
0-310-27103-7	*Your Time-Starved Marriage Groupware DVD*	DVD
0-310-27155-X	*Your Time-Starved Marriage Workbook for Men*	Softcover
0-310-26729-3	*Your Time-Starved Marriage Workbook for Women*	Softcover

Interested in hosting the Parrotts for one of their highly acclaimed seminars? It's easy. Just visit *www.RealRelationships.com* to learn more and complete a speaking request form.

Les and Leslie speak to thousands in dozens of cities annually. They are entertaining, thought-provoking, and immeasurably practical. One minute you'll be laughing and the next you'll sit still in silence as they open your eyes to how you can make your relationship all it's meant to be.

> "I've personally benefited from the Parrotts' seminar. You can't afford to miss it."
>
> Gary Smalley

> "Les and Leslie's seminars can make the difference between you having winning relationships and disagreeable ones."
>
> Zig Ziglar

> "The Parrotts will revolutionize your relationships."
>
> Josh McDowell

> "Without a doubt, Les and Leslie are the best at what they do and they will help you become a success where it counts most."
>
> John C. Maxwell

Learn more about the Parrotts' "Becoming
Soul Mates Seminar" and their new "Love Talk Seminar."

*Click on www.RealRelationships.com
to bring them to your community.*

Love Talk
Speak Each Other's Language Like You Never Have Before

Drs. Les and Leslie Parrott

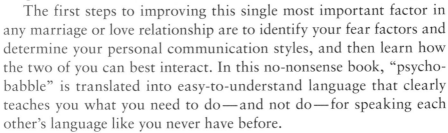

A breakthrough discovery in communication for transforming love relationships.

Over and over, couples consistently name "improved communication" as the greatest need in their relationships. *Love Talk* — by acclaimed relationship experts Drs. Les and Leslie Parrott — is a deep yet simple plan full of new insights that will revolutionize communication in love relationships.

The first steps to improving this single most important factor in any marriage or love relationship are to identify your fear factors and determine your personal communication styles, and then learn how the two of you can best interact. In this no-nonsense book, "psycho-babble" is translated into easy-to-understand language that clearly teaches you what you need to do — and not do — for speaking each other's language like you never have before.

Love Talk includes:

- The Love Talk Indicator, a free personalized online assessment (a $30.00 value) to help you determine your unique talk style
- The Secret to Emotional Connection
- Charts and sample conversations
- The most important conversation you'll ever have
- A short course on Communication 101
- Appendix on Practical Help for the "Silent Partner"

Two softcover "his and hers" workbooks are full of lively exercises and enlightening self-tests that help couples apply what they are learning about communication directly to their relationships.

Hardcover   0-310-24596-6

Also Available:

ISBN	Title	Format
0-310-80381-0	*Just the Two of Us*	Hardcover
0-310-26214-3	*Love Talk*	Audio CD, Abridged
0-310-20407-7	*Love Talk*	DVD
0-310-81047-7	*Love Talk Starters*	Mass Market
0-310-26212-7	*Love Talk Workbook for Men*	Softcover
0-310-26213-5	*Love Talk Workbook for Women*	Softcover

The Complete Guide to Marriage Mentoring

Connecting Couples to Build Better Marriages

Drs. Les and Leslie Parrott

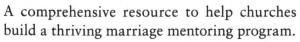

A comprehensive resource to help churches build a thriving marriage mentoring program.

Les and Leslie Parrott are passionate about how marriage mentoring can transform couples, families, and entire congregations. *The Complete Guide to Marriage Mentoring* includes life-changing insights and essential skills for

- Preparing engaged and newlywed couples
- Maximizing marriages from good to great
- Repairing marriages in distress

Practical guidelines help mentors and couples work together as a team, agree on outcomes, and develop skills for the marriage mentoring process. Appendixes offer a wealth of additional resources and tools. An exhaustive resource for marriage mentorship in any church setting, this guide also includes insights from interviews with church leaders and marriage mentors from around the country.

> "The time is ripe for marriage mentoring, and this book is exactly what we need."
>
> — Gary Smalley, author of **The DNA of Relationships**

Hardcover, Printed   0-310-27046-4

Also Available:

0-310-27047-2	*51 Creative Ideas for Marriage Mentors*	Softcover
0-310-27110-X	*Complete Resource Kit for Marriage Mentoring, The*	Curriculum Kit
0-310-27165-7	*Marriage Mentor Training Manual for Husbands*	Softcover
0-310-27125-8	*Marriage Mentor Training Manual for Wives*	Softcover

Pick up a copy today at your favorite bookstore!

ZONDERVAN®

GRAND RAPIDS, MICHIGAN 49530 USA

WWW.ZONDERVAN.COM

You Matter More Than You Think

What a Woman Needs to Know about the Difference She Makes

Dr. Leslie Parrott

Am I making a difference?

Does my life matter?

"How can I make a difference when some days I can't even find my keys?" asks award-winning author Leslie Parrott. "I've never been accused of being methodical, orderly, or linear. So when it came to considering my years on this planet, I did so without a sharpened pencil and a pad of paper. Instead, I walked along Discovery Beach, just a few minutes from our home in Seattle.

"Strange, though. All I seemed to ever bring home from my walks on the beach were little pieces of sea glass. Finding these random pieces eventually became a fixation. And, strangely, with each piece I collected, I felt a sense of calm. What could this mean? What was I to discover from this unintentional collection?"

In this poignant and vulnerable book, Leslie shows you how each hodgepodge piece of your life, no matter how haphazard, represents a part of what you do and who you are. While on the surface, none of these pieces may seem to make a terribly dramatic impact, Leslie will show you how they are your life and how when they are collected into a jar — a loving human heart — they become a treasure.

Hardcover 0-310-24598-2

Pick up a copy today at your favorite bookstore!

GRAND RAPIDS, MICHIGAN 49530 USA

WWW.ZONDERVAN.COM

Saving Your Marriage Before It Starts

Seven Questions to Ask Before — and After — You Marry

Drs. Les and Leslie Parrott

A trusted marriage resource for engaged and newlywed couples is now expanded and updated.

With more than 500,000 copies in print, *Saving Your Marriage Before It Starts* has become the gold standard for helping today's engaged and newlywed couples build a solid foundation for lifelong love. Trusted relationship experts Drs. Les and Leslie Parrott offer seven time-tested questions to help couples debunk the myths of marriage, bridge the gender gap, fight a good fight, and join their spirits for a rock-solid marriage.

This expanded and updated edition of *Saving Your Marriage Before It Starts* has been honed by ten years of feedback, professional experience, research, and insight, making this tried-and-true resource better than ever. Specifically designed to meet the needs of today's couples, this book equips readers for a lifelong marriage before it even starts.

The men's and women's workbooks include self-tests and exercises sure to bring about personal insight and help you apply what you learn. The seven-session DVD features the Parrotts' lively presentation as well as real-life couples, making this a tool you can use "right out of the box." A bonus session for second marriages is also included. The unabridged audio CD is read by the authors.

The Curriculum Kit includes DVD with leader's guide, workbook for men, workbook for women, and hardcover book. All components, except for DVD, are also sold separately.

Curriculum Kit   0-310-27180-0

Also Available:
0-310-26210-0	*Saving Your Marriage Before It Starts*	Audio CD, Unabridged
0-310-26565-7	*Saving Your Marriage Before It Starts Workbook for Men*	Softcover
0-310-26564-9	*Saving Your Marriage Before It Starts Workbook for Women*	Softcover

We want to hear from you. Please send your comments about this
book to us in care of zreview@zondervan.com. Thank you.

GRAND RAPIDS, MICHIGAN 49530 USA

ZONDERVAN.COM/
AUTHORTRACKER